Ancient Greece Trivia

450 Engaging Questions and Answers to Test Your Knowledge of Greek History, Mythology, and Philosophy

Welcome Aboard, Check Out This Limited-Time Free Bonus!

Ahoy, reader! Welcome to the Ahoy Publications family, and thanks for snagging a copy of this book! Since you've chosen to join us on this journey, we'd like to offer you something special.

Check out the link below for a FREE e-book filled with delightful facts about American History.

But that's not all - you'll also have access to our exclusive email list with even more free e-books and insider knowledge. Well, what are ye waiting for? Click the link below to join and set sail toward exciting adventures in American History.

Access your bonus here
https://ahoypublications.com/
Or, Scan the QR code!

Table of Contents

Introduction

Are you ready to explore the fascinating history of ancient Greece? From the Minoan and Mycenaean civilizations to Homeric poetry and Sparta and Athens' rise in power until their decline during the Roman occupation, this book will guide you through all these topics and more.

Discover how the Greek alphabet was invented, learn about its impact on society, find out what made Athenian democracy unique under Cleisthenes' rule, and follow Alexander the Great throughout his conquests that marked the era known as the Hellenistic age.

Follow us also into religion, mythology, philosophy, art, and culture—uncovering some of the most intriguing mysteries surrounding ancient Greece. Unravel myths such as Troy's legendary fall and appreciate one of the world's most renowned monuments, the Acropolis, with its magnificent buildings built during Pericles' reign. Dive deep into the Greco-Roman cultural exchange that shaped much of our modern-day lives, its impact on the spread of Christianity, and how it all ended with barbarian invasions.

So, what are you waiting for? Let's start our journey through ancient Greece.

Minoan Civilization

Welcome to the chapter on the Minoan civilization, an ancient culture that spanned from around 3200 BC to 1200 BC. In this chapter, you'll test your knowledge of this captivating civilization with trivia questions ranging from who discovered major cities in Crete to techniques used in architecture during this era that led the Minoans to create. You'll explore their mastery over pottery making, represented through artifacts that have been uncovered in ruins today, and their transport systems based around waterways throughout nearby islands.

1. During which age did the Minoan civilization thrive?

    a. Iron Age   c. Bronze Age

    b. Copper Age   d. Stone Age

2. Where did the Minoans live?

    a. Peloponnese

    b. Egypt

    c. Crete

    d. Phoenicia

3. Who discovered Knossos, one of the major cities in ancient Crete and part of the Minoan civilization?

    a. Sir Arthur Evans

    b. Howard Carter

    c. Heinrich Schliemann

    d. None of the above

4. Which was the most prominent art form during this period?

    a. Pottery

    b. Sculpture

    c. Painting

    d. Frescoes

5. How many palaces have been discovered in Crete by archaeologists?

    a. One

    b. Three

    c. Five

    d. Seven

6. Which of these writing systems did the Minoans develop?

    a. Linear A

    b. Linear B

    c. Cretan hieroglyphs

    d. Both a and c

7. Which of these ancient cultures did not have regular contact with the Minoan civilization?

    a. Egypt

    b. Rome

    c. Phoenicia

    d. None of the above

8. In which century did the decline of Minoan civilization begin?

    a. Eleventh century BC

    b. Fifteenth century BC

    c. Eighteenth century BC

    d. Twenty-first century BC

9. Who were the rulers of the Minoan civilization during its peak period?

    a. Priests

    b. Kings

    c. Warriors

    d. We don't know for sure

10. How did the Minoan civilization most likely collapse?

 a. Invasion by Mycenaeans

 b. Plague

 c. Volcano eruption

 d. All of the above

11. Which of these is not an archeological site that belongs to the Minoan civilization?

 a. Knossos

 b. Phaistos

 c. Athens

 d. Zakros

12. What does the term "amphora" refer to with regards to the Minoan civilization?

 a. A type of pottery

 b. A type of theater building

 c. A type of naval vessel

 d. None of the above

13. What color was mostly used to decorate the palace of Knossos?

 a. White

 b. Blue

 c. Red

 d. Yellow

14. Which is the second largest Minoan palace discovered so far?

 a. Phaistos

 b. Knossos

 c. Hagia Triada

 d. Zakros

15. Which of these was the main source of income in the Minoan civilization's economy?

 a. Farming

 b. Fishing

 c. Mining

 d. Trading

16. Which types of events were depicted in some wall paintings found in Knossos?

a. Religious ceremonies

b. Naval battles

c. Athletic competitions

d. All of the above

17. What is considered one of the most famous artifacts from this period?

a. The Mask of Agamemnon

b. Aphrodite's Mirror

c. Bull-Leaping Fresco

d. None of the above

18. What type of clothing are men and women seen wearing in frescoes and statues from this period?

a. Togas

b. Tunics

c. Kimonos

d. Chitons

19. Which of these was a sacred being for the Minoans?

a. Squirrel

b. Dolphin

c. Cat

d. Bull

20. Minoan fresco painters worked on frescoes in which ancient civilization's cities?

a. Rome

b. Mesopotamia

c. Egypt

d. Scythia

ANSWERS

1. c. Bronze Age
2. c. Crete
3. a. Sir Arthur Evans
4. a. Pottery
5. c. Five
6. d. Both a and c
7. b. Rome
8. b. Fifteenth century BC
9. d. We don't know for sure
10. c. Volcano eruption
11. c. Athens
12. a. A type of pottery
13. c. Red
14. a. Phaistos
15. d. Trading
16. a. Religious ceremonies
17. c. Bull-Leaping Fresco
18. d. Chitons
19. d. Bull
20. c. Egypt

Mycenaean Civilization

Explore the world of ancient Greece and discover facts about one of history's most influential civilizations: the Mycenaean, an exciting period to unravel with trivia questions. What was the location of this civilization? Who were some of the significant leaders of this era? What kind of writing system were they using to exchange messages? Learn the answers to all these questions and more as we take a deep dive into life in the Mycenaean civilization.

21. What is the approximate date range of the Mycenaean civilization?

    a. 2000–1500 BC

    b. 200–1000 BC

    c. 1750–1050 BC

    d. 1400–1300 BC

22. What is Mycenae, which the Mycenaean civilization is named after?

    a. Another name for Greece

    b. The most important site of the civilization

    c. A type of pottery found in the region

    d. None of the above

23. Who were some important rulers during this period?

    a. Agamemnon, Menelaus, Paris, and Achilles

    b. Homer, Plato, Socrates, and Aristotle

    c. Alexander the Great, Darius III, and Cyrus II

    d. Pericles, Solon, Cleisthenes, and Pisistratus

24. What type of writing system did the Mycenaeans use to communicate?

a. Linear A script

b. Greek Alphabet

c. Linear B

d. Babylonian Cuneiform

25. What type of economy did the Mycenaean civilization have?

a. A palace economy regulated by the rulers

b. A simple hunter-gatherer economy

c. A slave trade economy

d. An agriculture-based economy

26. Which famous Greek myth is said to have taken place in this period?

a. The *Iliad*

b. Theseus and Minotaur

c. Heracles' Twelve Labors

d. None of the above

27. Which of these was not a Mycenaean city?

a. Mycenae

b. Troy

c. Tiryns

d. Pylos

28. Which social class was at the top of the Mycenaean hierarchy?

a. Priests

b. Merchants

c. Warriors

d. Artisans

29. What does the term *wanax* signify?

a. Sword

b. Soldier

c. King

d. Money

30. Other than Greece and the Aegean islands, where were some of the Mycenaean settlements located?

a. North Africa

b. Anatolia

c. South Italy

d. None of the above

31. What were the main contingents in the Mycenaean armies?

a. Heavy infantry

b. Cavalry

c. Javelin men

d. Slingers

32. What term refers to the type of architecture found in Mycenaean cities?

a. Beehive

b. Minotaurean

c. Cyclopean

d. Doric

33. Which of these is not true of the Mycenaean civilization?

a. The Mycenaeans were ruled by kings

b. The Mycenaeans traded extensively in the Mediterranean

c. The Mycenaeans defeated the Latins many times

d. All statements are true

34. Which of these was not a common export of the Mycenaeans during this period?

a. Olives

b. Iron weapons

c. Pottery

d. Wine

35. Which of these was a chief deity for the Mycenaeans?

a. Zeus

b. Ares

c. Poseidon

d. Bacchus

36. What is the megaron, found in the Mycenaean palaces?

    a. Throne room

    b. Circular tower

    c. Main column of the entrance

    d. Back gate of the palace

37. What is one of the most iconic pieces of Mycenaean warrior equipment?

    a. Pikes

    b. Square shields

    c. Boar-tusk helmets

    d. All of the above

38. Which ancient artifact is sometimes referred to as the "Mona Lisa of prehistory"?

    a. Mask of Agamemnon

    b. Sword of Achilles

    c. Hammer of Hector

    d. Toga of Odysseus

39. What type of burial practices were used by this civilization?

    a. Cremation

    b. Mummification

    c. Shaft graves

    d. None of the above

40. Which of these was the main factor behind the decline of the Mycenaean civilization?

    a. Volcanic eruption

    b. Invasion by the Sea Peoples

    c. Civil war

    d. Slave uprising

ANSWERS

21. c. 1750–1050 BC

22. b. The most important site of the civilization

23. a. Agamemnon, Menelaus, Paris, and Achilles

24. c. Linear B

25. a. A palace economy regulated by the rulers

26. a. The *Iliad*

27. b. Troy

28. c. Warriors

29. c. King

30. b. Anatolia

31. a. Heavy infantry

32. c. Cyclopean

33. c. The Mycenaeans defeated the Latins many times

34. b. Iron weapons

35. c. Poseidon

36. a. Throne room

37. c. Boar-tusk helmets

38. a. Mask of Agamemnon

39. c. Shaft graves

40. b. Invasion by the Sea Peoples

Greek Dark Ages: Migration and Settlement Patterns

During the Greek Dark Ages, foundational elements of modern-day Greece were established as population displacement and migrations caused major changes to regional settlement patterns. This chapter explores what drove these migrations and their impacts on social structures, economic activity, cultural development, and warfare practices. You'll discover how ensuing tribal organizations led to today's political standings. The chapter also includes questions about who was responsible for the destruction of important Mycenaean palaces.

41. **What was the main cause of migration and settlement patterns during the Greek Dark Ages?**

    a. Economic opportunities

    b. Climate change

    c. Political instability

    d. Military conflicts

42. **Which event marks the start of the Greek Dark Ages?**

    a. The Fall of Troy

    b. The Battle of Marathon

    c. The Peloponnesian War

    d. The Late Bronze Age collapse

43. Until when did the Greek Dark Ages last?

    a. 1000 BC

    b. 900 BC

    c. 800 BC

    d. 500 BC

44. Who were the Dorians?

    a. Phoenician travelers

    b. A Greek ethnic group

    c. Servants of the king Dori

    d. None of the above

45. What was one of the main consequences of the Greek Dark Ages?

    a. Increased wealth and prosperity

    b. Decline in population growth

    c. Increase in trade and commerce

    d. Destruction of Troy

46. How did migration during this period affect culture within Greece?

    a. It led to increased cultural diversity

    b. It led to decreased cultural diversity

    c. It did not affect cultural diversity

    d. None of the above

47. What happened to the Linear B script used by the Greeks during the Greek Dark Ages?

    a. It was developed into Linear C

    b. It ceased being used

    c. It was modified according to Phoenician scripts

    d. It was spread to Italy

48. What was the fate of the Mycenaean palatial society during the Greek Dark Ages?

    a. Its centers were destroyed

    b. Palatial society was transformed into an oligarchy

    c. A slave rebellion put an end to the palaces

    d. A foreign despot united all Mycenaean centers

49. Which group is believed to have been responsible for the destruction of many Mycenaean palaces?
    a. The Dorians
    b. The Minoans
    c. The Ionians
    d. The Hittites
50. Who were some notable individuals who migrated and settled in new regions during this period?
    a. Agamemnon, Achilles, and Odysseus
    b. Paris, Priam, and Hector
    c. Pausanias, Cimon, and Pericles
    d. None of the above
51. What type of settlements were dominant during the Greek Dark Ages?
    a. Small rural villages
    b. Large cities
    c. Military fortresses
    d. Nomadic encampments
52. How did migration influence economic activity in Greece in this period?
    a. It led to increased specialization of labor
    b. It did not affect economic activity
    c. It caused a decrease in trade and commerce
    d. It replaced local economies with foreign ones
53. Which group is credited for introducing the use of iron in Greece?
    a. The Dorians
    b. The Ionians
    c. The Hittites
    d. The Scythians
54. What was one major consequence of migrations during this period in terms of cultural development?
    a. Increased literacy rate
    b. Decline in technological advancement
    c. The emergence of new religious cults
    d. Evolutionary stagnation

55. In what way did population displacement affect social structures within Greece during this period?

a. It led to increased social stratification

b. It created a more egalitarian society

c. It did not affect existing societal structures

d. It caused the breakdown of traditional hierarchies

56. Which of these ancient civilizations also experienced a period of decline after the Late Bronze Age collapse?

a. Colchis

b. Egypt

c. Rome

d. China

57. Which of these pottery styles was prominent during the Greek Dark Ages?

a. Protogeometric pottery

b. Orientalizing style pottery

c. Geometric pottery

d. Black-figure pottery

58. How were settlement patterns impacted by migration during this period?

a. There was an increase in urbanization.

b. Migrants tended to settle near coastlines.

c. Settlements clustered around rivers and mountains.

d. None of the above

59. Who are regarded as some major contributors to Greek culture during this period?

a. Thales

b. Solon

c. Homer

d. None of the above

60. What were the Greek *oikoi*?

a. Farmland plots on the Peloponnese

b. New type of clay pots used in the Dark Ages

c. An elite military unit

d. Early Greek households

ANSWERS

41. b. Climate change

42. d. The Late Bronze Age collapse

43. c. 800 BC

44. b. A Greek ethnic group

45. b. Decline in population growth

46. a. It led to increased cultural diversity

47. b. It ceased being used

48. a. Its centers were destroyed

49. a. The Dorians

50. d. None of the above

51. a. Small rural villages

52. c. It caused a decrease in trade and commerce

53. a. The Dorians

54. b. Decline in technological advancement

55. d. It caused the breakdown of traditional hierarchies

56. b. Egypt

57. a. Protogeometric pottery

58. b. Migrants tended to settle near coastlines.

59. d. None of the above

60. d. Early Greek households

The Trojan War

This chapter of *Ancient Greece Trivia* introduces readers to some of the most well-known poets, warriors, gods, goddesses, and stories from ancient times. Embark on a journey into long ago with questions about the *Iliad* and the *Odyssey* written by Homer, the causes leading up to the ten-year war, who was responsible for killing Achilles, where Helen spent her honeymoon before marriage, what Odysseus used to escape Polyphemus' cave, whose funeral pyre was lit by one particular hero in the *Iliad*, and who gave fate-altering gifts such as arrows, horses, and spears during Troy's fall—plus much more.

61. According to Homer, what was the cause of the Trojan War?

   a. A dispute between Agamemnon and Menelaus over Helen of Troy

   b. The fall of Troy due to a giant wooden horse left by Greeks

   c. Zeus punishing Paris for his arrogance

   d. Achilles' anger at being dishonored by Agamemnon

62. When was the *Iliad* written?

   a. Eighth century BC

   b. Twelfth century AD

   c. Fifth century BC

   d. Seventeenth century AD

63. In which language were the original versions of the *Iliad* and the *Odyssey* written?

a. Latin

b. Ancient Greek

c. Arabic

d. Phoenician

64. What was the name of Achilles' immortal horse?

a. Pegasus

b. Xanthus

c. Odysseus

d. Agamemnon

65. Where did Helen of Troy live before she married Menelaus, King of Sparta?

a. Troy

b. Athens

c. Sparta

d. Argos

66. The gods on Olympus played an important role in determining the outcome of battles during the Trojan War. Which goddess had special jurisdiction over warfare and strategy?

a. Athena

b. Eris

c. Hera

d. Aphrodite

67. How did the Trojan War end?

a. The Greeks emerged victorious

b. The Trojans won the war

c. Both sides signed a peace treaty

d. The war is said to have no definitive end

68. Who killed Hector in battle, according to Homer's *Iliad*?

a. Agamemnon

b. Ajax

c. Achilles

d. Odysseus

69. What does the word *kleos* signify as a major theme in both epics?

a. Strength

b. Virtue

c. Glory

d. Zeal

70. According to a prophecy, who would be responsible for killing Achilles during the Trojan War?

a. Apollo

b. Ajax

c. Diomedes

d. Paris

71. In the *Odyssey*, where did Calypso keep Odysseus captive for seven years?

a. Crete

b. Ogygia

c. Olympus

d. Ithaca

72. Who is the author of the *Odyssey*?

a. Homer

b. Hesiod

c. Aeschylus

d. Sophocles

73. What did Odysseus use to escape from Polyphemus' cave?

a. A ten-meter spear

b. Arrow of Athena

c. A wooden horse

d. Bellies of the monster's sheep

74. How long did it take for Menelaus to return home after the Trojan War?

a. Ten years

b. Two days

c. Three months

d. Eight years

75. Which archeologist discovered the true ancient site of Troy?

  a. Heinrich Schliemann

  b. Howard Carter

  c. Arthur Evans

  d. Louis Leakey

76. Who helped Odysseus build his raft before leaving Calypso's island?

  a. Hades

  b. Hermes

  c. Poseidon

  d. Hera

77. What was the most important weapon that Achilles used during the Trojan War?

  a. His spear

  b. His shield

  c. His bow

  d. His sword

78. According to Homer, who lit the funeral pyre for Patroclus after he died in battle?

  a. Ajax

  b. Agamemnon

  c. Priam

  d. Achilles

79. How long did it take Odysseus to travel from Troy back home to Ithaca?

  a. Ten years

  b. One year

  c. Three months

  d. Seven years

80. Who was Agamemnon?

  a. Achilles' father

  b. King of the Mycenae

  c. Trojan soldier

  d. Brother of Paris

ANSWERS

61. a. A dispute between Agamemnon and Menelaus over Helen of Troy
62. a. Eighth century BC
63. b. Ancient Greek
64. b. Xanthus
65. c. Sparta
66. a. Athena
67. a. The Greeks emerged victorious
68. c. Achilles
69. c. Glory
70. d. Paris
71. b. Ogygia
72. a. Homer
73. d. Bellies of the monster's sheep
74. d. Eight years
75. a. Heinrich Schliemann
76. b. Hermes
77. a. His spear
78. d. Achilles
79. a. Ten years
80. b. King of the Mycenae

Homeric Hymns and Oral Poetry Tradition

With this chapter on Homeric Hymns and oral poetic traditions, you can fully immerse yourself in the history of ancient Greece. Examine your understanding or pick up some new skills as you delve into the rich history of oral poetry, which has its roots in Greece. Find out what prompted this epic poetry. Trace the progression from oral recitation to transcription into manuscripts. Find out how many hymns from more than 2,000 years ago still survive and why some of them are still so relevant. With questions covering everything from Homer's epic writing style to the emphasis of the Homeric Hymn "To Hermes," this trivia quiz is jam-packed with information. Best of luck.

81. What is the term for the meter used in Homer's style of epic composition?

    a. Hexameter

    b. Iambic pentameter

    c. Monometer

    d. Dactylic hexameter

82. Which of these authors utilized Homeric Greek in their writings?

    a. Socrates

    b. Hesiod

    c. Virgil

    d. Plato

83. How many Homeric Hymns were created and survive today?
    a. Ten
    b. Fourteen
    c. Twenty-five
    d. Thirty-three

84. Which theme was commonly used by poets during the oral poetry tradition?
    a. Love stories
    b. War tales
    c. Adventure narratives
    d. All of the above

85. Where does most of our knowledge about Homeric Hymns come from?
    a. Ancient manuscripts
    b. Archaeological finds
    c. Orally transmitted folklore
    d. None of the above

86. What is the main topic of the Homeric Hymns?
    a. The aftermath of the Trojan War
    b. Appraisal of individual gods from the Greek pantheon
    c. Events of the Peloponnesian War
    d. Ancient love stories

87. Where does the Homeric Hymn "To Apollo" mainly take place?
    a. Athens and Sparta
    b. Sparta and Corinth
    c. Corinth and Delphi
    d. Delphi and Delos

88. When were the Homeric Hymns first published in print?
    a. Fifteenth century CE
    b. Sixteenth century CE
    c. Seventeenth century CE
    d. Twentieth century CE

89. Which of these Homeric Hymn contains the most surviving lines?

    a. "To Dionysus"

    b. "To Apollo"

    c. "To Hermes"

    d. "To Zeus"

90. How many books are there in the *Odyssey*?

    a. Four

    b. Ten

    c. Twenty-four

    d. Eighteen

91. In ancient Greek literature, what does the theme of *nostos* signify?

    a. Return to home

    b. Tragic war

    c. Revenge

    d. Failed love

92. About how many lines are there in the *Odyssey*?

    a. 12,000

    b. 7,000

    c. 16,000

    d. 21,000

93. What is the main topic of the Homeric Hymn "To Demeter"?

    a. Athena's wisdom and craftsmanship

    b. Hera's struggle for power

    c. Apollo's music

    d. Persephone's abduction

94. Which hymn gives the origin of the sacred ritual known as the Eleusinian Mysteries?

    a. "To Dionysus"

    b. "To Aphrodite"

    c. "To Demeter"

    d. "To Apollo"

95. Which hymn features the Delian Festival?

a. "To Hermes"

b. "To Apollo"

c. "To Poseidon"

d. "To Aphrodite"

ANSWERS

81. d. Dactylic hexameter

82. b. Hesiod

83. d. Thirty-three

84. d. All of the above

85. a. Ancient manuscripts

86. b. Appraisal of individual gods from the Greek pantheon

87. d. Delphi and Delos

88. a. Fifteenth century CE

89. c. Hermes

90. c. Twenty-four

91. a. Return to home

92. a. 12,000

93. d. Persephone's abduction

94. c. "To Demeter"

95. b. "To Apollo"

Rise of Sparta and Athens

The history of ancient Greece in many ways shaped the Western world we know today. While numerous city-states rose and fell, few left such a lasting impression as Sparta and Athens. This chapter explores these two ancient cities with questions regarding their rise to power, key differences, contributions to philosophy, government structures, and military strength. With questions about Solon's reforms in Athens and more, see how much you can remember from your study of ancient Greek history.

96. What type of political organization did Athens and Sparta constitute?

    a. Empire

    b. Protectorate

    c. City-state

    d. Kingdom

97. Who was the founder and the main reformer of Spartan society as we know it today?

    a. Lycurgus

    b. Aristotle

    c. Pericles

    d. Herodotus

98. What type of government did Sparta have during most of its existence?

a. Monarchy

b. Theocracy

c. Oligarchy

d. Democracy

99. During antiquity, which city-state had the most population?

a. Athens

b. Corinth

c. Argos

d. Sparta

100. What were the Spartans best known for?

a. Their democracy

b. Their metallurgy

c. Their military prowess

d. All of the above

101. What is the period in Greece between about the eighth century BC and the fifth century BC known as?

a. Classical Greece

b. Archaic Greece

c. Greek Dark Ages

d. Post-classical Greece

102. Who was Solon?

a. Athenian statesman and lawmaker

b. Most successful Athenian general

c. The last king of Athens

d. All of the above

103. How many classes were there in Spartan society?

a. Two

b. Three

c. Four

d. Five

104. What type of education did boys receive in Sparta?

a. Military training only

b. Academic and military training

c. Academic only

d. No formal education

105. Which philosopher proposed theories on democracy, justice, and virtue based on his time living in Athens?

a. Protagoras

b. Socrates

c. Pythagoras

d. Demosthenes

106. When did the Second Messenian War take place?

a. 700-685 BC

b. 660-650 BC

c. 600-595 BC

d. 590-585 BC

107. Which of the following is not true about Sparta?

a. It was an agrarian society

b. Its citizens were allowed to own land

c. Slaves formed the majority of its population

d. Women had the same rights as men

108. Who emerged victorious from the Second Messenian War?

a. Athens

b. Knossos

c. Sparta

d. Macedon

109. What were hoplites in Sparta?

a. The ruling class

b. Heavy infantry soldiers

c. Elite cavalry troops

d. Lightly armed scouts

110. Who wrote *History of the Peloponnesian War?*

a. Herodotus

b. Thucydides

c. Plato

d. Aristotle

111. When did the earthquake take place that destroyed much of Sparta and other cities of the Peloponnese?

a. 579 BC

b. 527 BC

c. 480 BC

d. 464 BC

112. How was the Athenian political system different from that of other city-states?

a. It was a direct democracy

b. It allowed citizens to vote

c. It had elected officials

d. All of the above

113. What was the main purpose of democracy for the Athenians?

a. To protect their interests from foreign powers

b. To ensure citizens were involved in government decisions

c. To create laws that favored only certain classes

d. None of the above

114. Who were the Agiads and the Eurypontids?

a. Peloponnesian tribes

b. Two major political parties in Athens

c. Spartan ruling families

d. None of the above

115. What was the agoge?

a. Spartan education program

b. Name of the main palace of Sparta

c. Athens' legal system

d. None of the above

ANSWERS

96. c. City-state

97. a. Lycurgus

98. c. Oligarchy

99. a. Athens

100. c. Their military prowess

101. b. Archaic Greece

102. a. Athenian statesman and lawmaker

103. b. Three

104. a. Military training

105. b. Socrates

106. b. 660-650 BC

107. d. Women had the same rights as men

108. c. Sparta

109. b. Heavy infantry soldiers

110. b. Thucydides

111. d. 464 BC

112. d. All of the above

113. b. To ensure citizens were involved in government decisions

114. c. Spartan ruling families

115. a. Spartan education program

The Invention of the Greek Alphabet

Since the dawn of human civilization, written language has been a powerful tool used to record and share knowledge. One of the most famous early writing systems is the alphabet, which originated in ancient Greece almost 3,000 years ago. In this chapter of *Ancient Greek Trivia*, we'll explore these and other questions: Who first invented the alphabet? How many letters were present in different versions of its adaptation? What purpose did the alphabet serve initially, and how was their version different from the Phoenicians' version? Read on to find out more about these intriguing discoveries.

116. What is the approximate time frame of the invention of the Greek alphabet?

    a. Fifth century BC

    b. Eighth century BC

    c. Tenth century BC

    d. Sixth century BC

117. From which civilization did the ancient Greeks adopt their alphabet?

    a. Egyptians

    b. Greeks

    c. Romans

    d. Phoenicians

118. Why did the ancient Greeks adopt a new alphabet at this time?

a. The old alphabet was too complex

b. They were conquered by a new dynasty

c. They had lost their writing system during the Greek Dark Ages

d. They voted to adopt it

119. What was included in the original Phoenician alphabet that made it easy for other nations to use and modify?

a. Vowels

b. Consonants

c. Symbols

d. Writing direction

120. How many letters are in the Greek version of the alphabet taken from the Phoenician model?

a. Twenty-four

b. Twenty-two

c. Twenty-six

d. Thirty-two

121. How did the Greeks improve upon their adaptation of the Phoenician alphabet?

a. By adding vowels

b. By making them all capital letters

c. By creating new symbols

d. By changing the order of the letters

122. Which major linguistic sub-group is the Phoenician language a part of?

a. Indo-European

b. West Semitic

c. East Semitic

d. Arabic

123. Which language is not derived from the ancient Greek alphabet?

a. English

b. Latin

c. Arabic

d. Russian

124. How many different versions of the Greek alphabet developed over time and why?

    a. Two, as each city-state had its own version

    b. Three, as there were three main dialects

    c. Four, because they added new symbols

    d. Six, because it spread quickly through Europe

125. Where was the early version of the alphabet, which was the closest to the original, used mostly?

    a. Peloponnese

    b. Thracia

    c. Crete

    d. Anatolia

126. How were the letters in the Greek alphabet written?

    a. From right to left

    b. From top to bottom

    c. Randomly

    d. From left to right

127. Which mythological figure was credited by Herodotus with introducing the ancient Greek alphabet from Phoenicia?

    a. Perseus

    b. Cadmus

    c. Pericles

    d. Hermes

128. What is the name of one of the oldest surviving archeological finds that features the use of the Greek alphabet?

    a. Cup of Zeus

    b. Dipylon Inscription

    c. Mask of Agamemnon

    d. None of the above

129. How many letters are in the original Phoenician alphabet?

    a. Twenty-four

    b. Twenty-two

    c. Sixteen

    d. Twelve

130. Where was Cadmus born according to Herodotus?

 a. Troy

 b. Carthage

 c. Phoenicia

 d. Egypt

ANSWERS

116. b. Eighth century BC

117. d. Phoenicians

118. c. They had lost their old writing system during the Greek Dark Ages

119. b. Consonants

120. a. Twenty-four

121. a. By adding vowels

122. b. West Semitic

123. c. Arabic

124. c. Four, because they added new symbols

125. c. Crete

126. d. From left to right

127. b. Cadmus

128. b. Dipylon Inscription

129. b. Twenty-two

130. c. Phoenicia

Development of the Ancient Olympic Games

The Olympic Games were more than merely sports competitions in ancient Greece. For the people of that era, they were deeply significant both culturally and spiritually. Who established these historical events, then? That's still a mystery today. Many centuries later, societies all over the world have competed in the Olympics at different levels, with athletes from all walks of life taking part. Come explore one of the most significant turning points in human evolution that has produced a worldwide cultural phenomenon: the development of the ancient Olympic Games.

131. When were the first ancient Olympic Games?

    a. 776 BC

    b. 478 BC

    c. 393 AD

    d. 1200 BC

132. In ancient Greek mythology, who is credited with creating the Olympic Games?

    a. Poseidon

    b. Heracles

    c. Cronus

    d. Hera

133. According to ancient Greek mythology, who built the Olympic Stadium to honor Zeus?

a. Pelops

b. Achilles

c. Heracles

d. Apollo

134. How many sports were part of the original Olympic program?

a. Four

b. Five

c. Six

d. Seven

135. Who was the first Olympic champion according to tradition?

a. Heracles

b. Coroebus

c. Eliados

d. Ajax

136. Which of these was not one of the original disciplines in the Olympics?

a. Swimming

b. Wrestling

c. Long jump

d. Discus throw

137. What were the winning athletes awarded with?

a. Olive leaf wreaths

b. Gold armor

c. Commemorative necklaces

d. All of the above

138. What was the gymnasion?

a. The system used to reward losers

b. The palace where the first Olympics were held

c. The training facility for athletes

d. None of the above

139. **What was one peculiarity about the ancient Olympic Games?**

a. All contestants competed naked

b. Free men could not compete

c. They sacrificed the losers to the gods

d. All of the above

140. **At its conception, for how many days did each Olympic festival last at Olympia?**

a. One day

b. Two days

c. Three days

d. Twelve days

141. **Where did most of the events during the ancient Olympics take place?**

a. Temple of Hera

b. Stadium of Olympus

c. Gymnasium of Pisa

d. Theatre of Dionysus

142. **Which god was honored during the ancient Olympics?**

a. Hercules

b. Apollo

c. Zeus

d. Athena

143. **Who could initially take part in the Olympics?**

a. Only representatives of the Greek city-states

b. Trained athletes from the Mediterranean

c. Greeks and invited athletes from Egypt

d. All of the above

144. **Under which Roman emperor did the Olympic Games most likely cease to be held?**

a. Nero

b. Marcus Aurelius

c. Constantine

d. Theodosius

145. **How often did the ancient Greeks hold their Olympic Games?**

    a. Once every four years

    b. Every five years

    c. Annually

    d. Biennially

146. **What animal was usually sacrificed to Zeus during the Olympics?**

    a. Bull

    b. Sheep

    c. Cow

    d. Horse

147. **For about how long did the ancient Olympic Games continue to be held?**

    a. 100 Years

    b. 200 Years

    c. 300 Years

    d. 1,000 Years

148. **What was the diaulos?**

    a. Ancient version of the 400-meter race

    b. Ancient version of the triathlon

    c. Ancient version of chariot riding

    d. Ancient version of wrestling

149. **Who was the first Olympic champion in boxing?**

    a. Coroebus

    b. Onomastus of Smyrna

    c. Arrhichion of Phigalia

    d. None of the above

150. **Which of these was not part of the ancient Olympic Games?**

    a. Two-horse chariot racing

    b. Running

    c. Boxing

    d. Tennis

ANSWERS

131. a. 776 BC
132. b. Heracles
133. c. Heracles
134. b. Five
135. b. Coroebus
136. a. Swimming
137. a. Olive leaf wreaths
138. c. The training facility for athletes
139. a. All contestants competed naked
140. a. One day
141. b. Stadium of Olympus
142. c. Zeus
143. a. Only representatives of the Greek city-states
144. d. Theodosius
145. a. Once every four years
146. a. Bull
147. d. 1,000 years
148. a. Ancient version of the 400-meter race
149. b. Onomastus of Smyrna
150. d. Tennis

Development of the Athenian Democracy

Athenian democracy is famous for its unique structure, eye for detail, and the legacy it represents. With an eye toward internal stability and social mobility for all citizens—regardless of gender or class—Athens enacted sweeping political changes that would reshape the political landscape of the city-state for generations to come and influence other civilizations. Through this chapter, we'll explore questions about how democracy arose in Athens and what institutions developed as cornerstones of Athenian society. Let's get started.

151. Which type of government preceded democracy in Athens?

a. Monarchy

b. Theocracy

c. Oligarchy

d. Tyranny

152. In what year did the reforms of Cleisthenes contribute to furthering democracy in Athens?

a. 508 BC

b. 514 BC

c. 500 BC

d. 496 BC

153. Which statesman is responsible for laying the foundations for Athenian democracy in the early sixth century BC?

a. Plato

b. Solon

c. Thales

d. Cleobulus

154. What was the name of the assembly that was set up in Athens for male citizens to discuss politics?

a. The Great Council

b. The Areopagus

c. The Ecclesia

d. Demarchy

155. How many powerful traditional clans or tribes had existed in Athens before Cleisthenes' reforms?

a. Two

b. Six

c. Eight

d. Twenty

156. Which statesman is credited with introducing a harsh legal system in the year 621 BC that set back the development of democracy in Athens?

a. Solon

b. Draco

c. Cleisthenes

d. Hippias

157. About how many members were there in the Ecclesia?

a. 1,000

b. 3,000

c. 6,000

d. 10,000

158. What was the primary purpose of the Areopagus?

a. To act as the final court of appeal

b. To advise on military strategy

c. To implement Cleisthenes' reforms

d. None of the above

159. What was the Boule?

    a. A special assembly of magistrates

    b. A special assembly that ran the city's daily affairs

    c. A special assembly of the most powerful families of Athens

    d. None of the above

160. Who expanded the membership of the Boule from 400 to 500 members?

    a. Draco

    b. Solon

    c. Cleisthenes

    d. Ephialtes

161. Who had access to public offices under Cleisthenes' reforms?

    a. Rich citizens

    b. Freeborn male citizens

    c. Freeborn female citizens

    d. All Athenian residents

162. What was the purpose of ostracism under Cleisthenes' reforms?

    a. To exile those deemed dangerous to society

    b. To limit religious influence

    c. To reduce poverty among the masses

    d. All of the above

163. How did Cleisthenes assign political power within Athens?

    a. He divided it between four classes

    b. He distributed it to the wealthy families

    c. He gave more power to ordinary citizens

    d. He set up two councils to rule jointly

164. Who were the archons?

    a. Members of the Ecclesia

    b. Chief magistrates of Athens

    c. Eldest members of the ruling families

    d. Special representatives of the citizens

165. Which reformer was responsible for weakening the Areopagus?

a. Solon

b. Cleisthenes

c. Aristotle

d. Ephialtes

166. Which tyrant briefly overthrew the democracy in Athens in 561 BC?

a. Hippias

b. Peisistratos

c. Ephialtes

d. Draco

167. Before the reforms of Solon, how many archons ruled Athens from the Areopagus?

a. Five

b. Ten

c. Nine

d. Thirteen

168. Before the development of democracy, which of these was the magistrate that functioned as the religious leader or high priest of Athenian society?

a. Eponymous archon

b. Archon basileus

c. Archon polemarch

d. None of the above

169. What was one key innovation introduced by Cleisthenes that enabled more people to be involved in political decisions and debates?

a. Abolition of slavery

b. Introduction of ostracism

c. Creation of deme-based political units

d. Expansion of voting rights beyond wealthy landowners

170. About how many officials were outright elected by popular vote in Athens?

a. One hundred

b. Five hundred

c. Seven hundred

d. One thousand

171. Before the development of democracy, which of these was the magistrate that functioned as the military leader of Athenian society?

a. Eponymous archon

b. Archon basileus

c. Archon polemarch

d. Strategos

172. About how much of the population of Athens were allowed to vote?

a. 10-20 percent

b. 30-40 percent

c. 40-50 percent

d. 60-70 percent

173. Which of these magistrates held the highest political office in ancient Athens?

a. Eponymous archon

b. Archon basileus

c. Archon polemarch

d. Archon imperator

174. After the reforms of Cleisthenes, citizens of at least what age could be elected to the Boule?

a. Twenty-one

b. Twenty-five

c. Thirty

d. Forty

175. What was the name of the popular tribunal in Athenian democracy?

a. Areopagus

b. Hellaia

c. Ecclesia

d. Juria

176. Which of these statesmen introduced the third major series of reforms to Athenian democracy?

a. Pericles

b. Ephialtes

c. Cleisthenes

d. Hippias

177. Who established the principle of sortition when choosing public office-holders in Athenian democracy?

a. Draco

b. Solon

c. Ephialtes

d. Cleisthenes

178. What was the name of the court system functioning in democratic Athens?

a. Dikasteria

b. Mesogeia

c. Medimnoi

d. None of the above

179. Who further reduced the power of the Areopagus in 461 BC to that of a criminal court?

a. Pericles

b. Ephialtes

c. Leonidas

d. Cleomenes

180. Who were the executives of the Boule?

a. Prytaneis

b. Phylarcs

c. Heliasts

d. Thesmothenai

ANSWERS

151. c. Oligarchy

152. b. 508 BC

153. b. Solon

154. c. The Ecclesia

155. b. Four

156. b. Draco

157. c. 6,000

158. a. To act as the final court of appeal

159. a. A special assembly that ran the city's daily affairs

160. c. Cleisthenes

161. b. Freeborn male citizens

162. a. To exile those deemed dangerous to society

163. c. He gave more power to ordinary citizens

164. b. Chief magistrates of Athens

165. a. Solon

166. b. Peisistratos

167. c. Nine

168. b. Archon basileus

169. c. Creation of deme-based political units

170. a. One hundred

171. c. Archon polemarch

172. a. 10-20 percent

173. a. Eponymous archon

174. c. Thirty

175. b. Hellaia

176. b. Ephialtes

177. d. Cleisthenes

178. a. Dikasteria

179. b. Ephialtes

180. a. Prytaneis

The Greco-Persian Wars: Marathon and Thermopylae

Step back in time with *Ancient Greece Trivia* to explore the events of the Greco-Persian Wars. Discover answers to questions such as which city-state organized and led the resistance against Persian forces at Marathon, who commanded allied Greek forces into battle at Thermopylae and Salamis, how many ships were brought by Xerxes I when he came to Greece, what strategy ultimately caused the Persians' failure in conquering the Greeks, and more. Test your knowledge on a range of key battles. Featuring questions on the topics of leadership, strategy, and outcomes from this period in history, this chapter will take you on a journey into the past!

181. What year did the Greco-Persian Wars begin?

    a. 499 BC

    b. 479 BC

    c. 590 BC

    d. 679 BC

182. What event caused the outbreak of the Greco-Persian Wars?

    a. Murder of Xerxes

    b. Assassination of Greek envoys at Ctesiphon

    c. The Ionian Revolt

    d. None of the above

183. **Which Greek city-state was responsible for organizing and leading the resistance against Persian forces at the Battle of Marathon?**

a. Athens

b. Sparta

c. Corinth

d. Thebes

184. **When did the Battle of Marathon take place?**

a. 492 BC

b. 490 BC

c. 485 BC

d. 482 BC

185. **How many allied Greek soldiers were killed in battle at Thermopylae?**

a. 10,000

b. 7,000

c. 3,000

d. 500

186. **Who led the allied Greek forces into battle at Thermopylae under Spartan command?**

a. King Xerxes I of Persia

b. King Leonidas of Sparta

c. King Darius I of Persia

d. Miltiades the Athenian

187. **When did the Battle of Thermopylae take place?**

a. 490 BC

b. 485 BC

c. 480 BC

d. 475 BC

188. **What was the outcome of the Battle of Marathon?**

a. The Persians were victorious

b. The Greeks were victorious

c. A stalemate was reached

d. The battle ended in a draw

189. In which Greek city did the Greek city-states agree to a confederate alliance in 481 BC?

a. Corinth

b. Sparta

c. Argos

d. Thebes

190. Who led the Persian forces in the Battle of Thermopylae?

a. Darius the Great

b. Cyrus the Great

c. Xerxes I

d. Xerxes II

191. What was the outcome of the naval battle at Artemisium in 480 BC?

a. The Greeks gained the advantage.

b. The Persians gained the advantage.

c. A stalemate was reached

d. It is unknown

192. How many ships did the Persians lose at the Battle of Artemisium?

a. 100

b. 400

c. 1,000

d. 1,500

193. Under which Persian ruler did the first invasion of Greece take place?

a. Cyrus the Great

b. Darius the Great

c. Xerxes

d. Xerxes II

194. Which of these cities was destroyed by the Persians during this leader's invasion?

a. Corinth

b. Pella

c. Sparta

d. None of the above

195. What was the name of the Greek solider who, according to tradition, ran forty-one kilometers from Marathon to Athens after the battle to break the news of the outcome of the battle to the Athenians?

a. Adeimantus

b. Cleonidas

c. Pericles

d. Pheidippides

196. Who led the Greek navy at the Battle of Salamis?

a. Miltiades

b. Themistocles

c. Leonidas

d. Climon

197. What was the outcome of the Battle of Salamis?

a. Total Persian victory

b. Total Greek victory

c. Disengagement from both sides

d. None of the above

198. What was the final land battle between the Greeks and the Persians during the second Persian invasion of Greece?

a. Thermopylae

b. Thessaly

c. Plataea

d. Artemisium

199. What was the result of the Battle of Mycale in 479 BC?

a. The Greeks were victorious

b. The Persians were victorious

c. A stalemate was reached

d. None of the above

200. What was the ruling Persian royal dynasty at the time of the Greco-Persian Wars?

a. Achaemenid dynasty

b. Sassanid dynasty

c. Arsacid dynasty

d. Pahlavi dynasty

201. When were the Greco-Persian Wars concluded?

a. 475 BC

b. 463 BC

c. 458 BC

d. 449 BC

202. Which city-state was the leader of the Delian League?

a. Athens

b. Sparta

c. Corinth

d. Sardis

203. What strategy did Greek forces use to delay the Persian forces at Thermopylae?

a. Set fire to their ships

b. Charge head-on into battle

c. Attack from the rear

d. Wait in defensive positions

204. At which battle did the Delian League decisively defeat the Persians in 466 BC?

a. Eurymedon

b. Byzantium

c. Sestos

d. Mycale

205. With which treaty did the Greco-Persian Wars come to an end?

a. Thirty Years' Peace

b. Callias

c. Philocrates

d. Antalcidas

ANSWERS

181. a. 499 BC

182. c. The Ionian Revolt

183. a. Athens

184. b. 490 BC

185. c. 3,000

186. b. King Leonidas of Sparta

187. c. 480 BC

188. b. The Greeks were victorious

189. a. Corinth

190. c. Xerxes I

191. b. The Persians gained the advantage.

192. b. 400

193. b. Darius the Great

194. d. None of the above

195. d. Pheidippides

196. b. Themistocles

197. b. Total Greek victory

198. c. Plataea

199. a. The Greeks were victorious

200. a. Achaemenid dynasty

201. d. 449 BC

202. a. Athens

203. d. Wait in defensive positions

204. a. Eurymedon

205. b. Callias

Pericles and the Athenian Hegemony

Travel back in time to ancient Greece and explore the history of one of its most prominent structures, the Athenian Acropolis. In this chapter, you'll learn about the various building projects and reforms initiated by Pericles that led to Athens' emergence as a local power after the end of the Greco-Persian Wars. Dive into these trivia questions to find out more about Athenian achievements during the middle of the fifth century.

206. What does the term *pentecontaetia* refer to in ancient Greek history?

   a. The fifty rulers of Athens

   b. The fifty-year period that marked the zenith of Athenian power

   c. The fifty magistrates that plotted to kill Pericles

   d. None of the above

207. Which factor was crucial in Athens emerging as a hegemony in ancient Greece after the end of the Greco-Persian Wars?

   a. Strong leadership

   b. Domination of smaller Greek states

   c. Economic power from trade and commerce

   d. All of the above

208. Which great Greek statesman was Pericles the deputy of before his rise to power?

a. Cleisthenes

b. Ephialtes

c. Clemon

d. None of the above

209. When was Pericles elected as the strategos of Athens?

a. 450 BC

b. 445 BC

c. 480 BC

d. 461 BC

210. Until when did Pericles hold his office?

a. 430 BC

b. 429 BC

c. 425 BC

d. 424 BC

211. What was the main aim of Pericles' reforms of the Athenian political system?

a. Extension of the franchise to slaves

b. Strengthening of the Areopagus

c. Increase of political equality among citizens

d. Abandonment of democracy

212. How did the Athenian democracy help the poor members of its society during Pericles' rule?

a. By giving financial assistance to war widows

b. By giving land grants to dispossessed citizens

c. By creating more jobs for the poor

d. All of the above

213. The leadership of which confederation allowed Athens to reach the height of its power in the middle of the fifth century?

a. Peloponnesian League

b. League of Corinth

c. Delian League

d. League of Athens

214. Before Pericles moved it to Athens, where had the treasury of the league been located?

a. Sparta

b. Corinth

c. Rhodes

d. Delos

215. Where was Athenian military power concentrated during this period?

a. In its elite archer force

b. In its powerful navy

c. In its vast spy network

d. In its heavy cavalry contingents

216. What was the main driving force behind the Athenian economy?

a. Trade and commerce

b. Agriculture

c. Mining

d. Slave trade

217. Which historian called Pericles the "first citizen of Athens"?

a. Thucydides

b. Livy

c. Herodotus

d. Tacitus

218. What can be said of Athenian culture during this period?

a. It was the "Golden Age of Athens"

b. Athenian culture declined significantly

c. There were no major development in Athenian culture

d. None of the above

219. The construction of which major Athenian monument began under Pericles?

a. Agora

b. Parthenon

c. Circus Maximus

d. Theater of Herodes

220. Which ancient architect, a friend of Pericles, contributed to the development of many Athenian monuments during this time?

a. Philon

b. Ictinus

c. Phidias

d. Daedalus

221. Which of the Seven Wonders of the Ancient World were constructed in the 430s?

a. The Colossus of Rhodes

b. The Great Pyramids of Giza

c. The Temple of Artemis

d. The Great Statue of Zeus

222. Who designed Propylaea, at the entrance to the Acropolis?

a. Phidias

b. Mnesicles

c. Ictinus

d. Hippocrates

223. When did construction work begin on the Acropolis during Pericles' rule?

a. 449 BC

b. 443 BC

c. 429 BC

d. 425 BC

224. According to Thucydides, why did Pericles give his famous Funeral Oration?

a. To mark the passing of a Spartan general

b. To honor his mentor, who had recently passed away

c. To honor those who had died in the war that year

d. None of the above

225. How did Pericles die?

a. He was assassinated

b. He died of natural causes

c. He died from fatal wounds

d. He contracted the plague

ANSWERS

206. b. The fifty-year period that marked the zenith of Athenian power

207. d. All of the above

208. b. Ephialtes

209. b. 445 BC

210. b. 429 BC

211. c. Increase of political equality among citizens

212. d. All of the above

213. c. Delian League

214. d. Delos

215. b. In its powerful navy

216. a. Trade and commerce

217. a. Thucydides

218. a. It was the "Golden Age of Athens"

219. b. Parthenon

220. c. Phidias

221. d. The Great Statue of Zeus

222. b. Mnesicles

223. a. 449 BC

224. c. To hold a public funeral for those who had died in the war that year

225. d. He contracted the plague

Peloponnesian War between Athens and Sparta

The Peloponnesian War between Athens and Sparta stands as one of the most significant events in ancient Greece's history. This conflict has long been studied by historians, though many questions remain unanswered about it to this day. The start of the Peloponnesian War was marked by a period of considerable tension between two powerful Greek city-states, Sparta and Athens. Who started the war? How did each side battle against one another? What were some of the tactics used? These are all interesting topics to explore when diving into ancient Greece's history. Let's take a closer look at trivia surrounding this massive rivalry.

226. Which of the following city-states was responsible for initiating the Peloponnesian War?

   a. Athens

   b. Sparta

   c. Thebes

   d. Corinth

227. What were Spartan hoplites known for in ancient Greece?

   a. Their expertise in naval warfare

   b. Their agility and use of archery tactics

   c. Their heavy armor and reliance on phalanx formations

   d. Their maneuverability on the battlefield

228. Which famous Athenian general led his army during the first years of the war?

a. Themistocles

b. Pericles

c. Aristides

d. Thucydides

229. Who commanded a fleet that destroyed much of an Athenian armada at Aegospotami in 405 BC?

a. Epaminondas

b. Lysander

c. Alcibiades

d. Brasidas

230. What event marked the start of the Peloponnesian War?

a. The assassination of Brasidas

b. The Athenian siege of Potidaea

c. The invasion of Athens

d. None of the above

231. Which city-state held more power before the outbreak of the war, according to historian Thucydides?

a. Sparta

b. Athens

c. They were equal in power

d. None of the above

232. In what year did the Peloponnesian War come to an end?

a. 431 BC

b. 404 BC

c. 429 BC

d. 425 BC

233. Who was the king of Sparta during the first years of the war?

a. Cleomenes I

b. Pausanias

c. Agesilaus II

d. Archidamus III

234. What was the biggest strength of Athens at the outbreak of the war?

a. Its heavy infantry

b. Its flexible democracy

c. Its wealth from its vassals

d. Its defensive fortifications in Attica

235. What was the treaty that ended the first phase of the war?

a. Peace of Nicias

b. Treaty of Delos

c. Thirty Years' Peace

d. Peace of Plataea

236. When was this peace treaty signed?

a. 433 BC

b. 429 BC

c. 421 BC

d. 415 BC

237. Who wrote an account about the Peloponnesian War in his work *History of The Peloponnesian War*?

a. Thucydides

b. Herodotus

c. Xenophon

d. Pausanias

238. How long did the first peace between Sparta and Athens last?

a. Three years

b. Six years

c. Seven years

d. Nine years

239. When did a plague strike Athens, weakening the city-state and killing tens of thousands of its inhabitants?

a. 421 BC

b. 429 BC

c. 430 BC

d. 413 BC

240. Which Athenian statesman supported a more aggressive policy in the war against Sparta?

a. Lysander

b. Pericles

c. Cleisthenes

d. Cleon

241. Who emerged victorious from the Battle of Pylos in 425 BC?

a. Sparta

b. Athens

c. Peloponnesian League

d. Neither side

242. Where did Athens launch a military expedition in 415-413 BC?

a. Anatolia

b. Sicily

c. Peloponnese

d. Crete

243. Which city-state was the most powerful ally of Sparta during the Peloponnesian War?

a. Pella

b. Delphi

c. Corinth

d. Rhodes

244. What was the name of the alliance of Greek city-states that jointly fought in the war against Athens?

a. Peloponnesian League

b. Delian League

c. Ionian League

d. Achaean League

245. What event further weakened Athens in 411 BC?

a. A coup

b. An earthquake

c. A plague

d. None of the above

246. Which power joined the war effort against Athens in 414 BC?

a. Egypt

b. Corinth

c. Persia

d. Rome

247. When did the naval Battle of Syme take place?

a. 415 BC

b. 414 BC

c. 412 BC

d. 411 BC

248. In which region were most of the Athenian allies located during the war?

a. Sicily

b. Peloponnese

c. The Aegean

d. Thrace

249. Which of these was the decisive battle of the Peloponnesian War that swung the tide in 405 BC?

a. Arginusae

b. Notium

c. Aegospotami

d. Cyprus

250. Who emerged victorious in the Peloponnesian War?

a. Persia

b. Sparta

c. Athens

d. Neither side

ANSWERS

226. b. Sparta

227. c. Their heavy armor and reliance on phalanx formations

228. b. Pericles

229. b. Lysander

230. b. The Athenian siege of Potidaea

231. b. Athens

232. b. 404 BC

233. d. Archidamus III

234. c. Its wealth from its vassals

235. a. Peace of Nicias

236. c. 421 BC

237. a. Thucydides

238. b. Six years

239. c. 430 BC

240. d. Cleon

241. b. Athens

242. b. Sicily

243. c. Corinth

244. a. Peloponnesian League

245. a. A coup

246. c. Persia

247. d. 411 BC

248. c. The Aegean

249. c. Aegospotami

250. b. Sparta

Alexander the Great's Conquest

Alexander the Great's conquests remain some of the most iconic in ancient Greek and world history. Upon ascending to power, he began his quest to spread Greek culture and language throughout Europe and Asia Minor and expand his empire's borders. Despite not living to see the completion of his great journey, he successfully conquered many territories and left an indelible legacy that persists today. How much do you know about Alexander's conquests and what followed after? Test your knowledge with this *Ancient Greece Trivia* chapter on Alexander's conquest.

251. When did Alexander the Great become the king of Macedon?

a. 486 BC

b. 336 BC

c. 323 BC

d. 300 BC

252. What was the main goal of Alexander's war against Persia?

a. To spread Greek culture and language throughout Europe and Asia Minor

b. To gain wealth for himself and expand his empire's borders

c. To conquer all lands east of Egypt

d. To avenge the death of his father, Philip II

253. How long did it take for Alexander to complete his conquest?

a. Two years

b. Four months

c. Ten years

d. Eighteen months

254. Where was Alexander born?

a. Sardis

b. Pella

c. Athens

d. Corinth

255. Who was the Alexander's tutor until he reached the age of sixteen?

a. Socrates

b. Plato

c. Aristotle

d. Diogenes

256. What was one result of Alexander's conquest?

a. The dissemination of Greek culture throughout Europe and Asia Minor

b. The creation of diverse cities reflective of multiple cultures

c. Increased trade among all civilizations

d. All of the above

257. When did the Battle of Issus take place?

a. 336 BC

b. 333 BC

c. 330 BC

d. 327 BC

258. Who led the forces of Persian at the Battle of Issus?

a. Alexander the Great

b. Darius II

c. Darius III

d. Darius IV

259. Which Greek city was destroyed during Alexander's campaign in Greece?

a. Corinth

b. Thebes

c. Sparta

d. Pella

260. Which alliance did Alexander emerge as the leader of after his conquest of the Greek city-states?

a. Peloponnesian League

b. League of Corinth

c. Ionian League

d. Thracian League

261. Which battle was Alexander's first victory against the Persians?

a. Issus

b. Granicus

c. Gaugamela

d. Miletus

262. When did Alexander conquer the city of Tyre?

a. 333 BC

b. 332 BC

c. 330 BC

d. 328 BC

263. How did Alexander's conquests affect religion?

a. He imposed Greek gods on conquered lands

b. He allowed freedom of worship

c. Religious conversion became mandatory

d. All religions were abolished

264. How was Alexander's conquest of Egypt met by the Egyptian people?

a. They resisted for years

b. They were too afraid to rise up against the ruthless conquerors

c. They treated Alexander as their liberator from the Persians

d. They managed to negotiate an alliance to avoid bloodshed

265. Who eventually succeeded Alexander as the ruler of Egypt after he died in Babylon?

a. Ptolemy I Soter

b. His son, Alex III

c. Olympias

d. Philip III

266. When did the Battle of Gaugamela take place?

a. 331 BC

b. 329 BC

c. 327 BC

d. 326 BC

267. After which battle did the Persian dynasty finally succumb to Alexander?

a. Gaugamela

b. Persian Gate

c. Ctesiphon

d. Issus

268. What was the name of one of Alexander's generals who had saved the king at the Battle of Granicus but was accidentally killed by a drunk Alexander in 328 BC?

a. Cleitus

b. Ptolemy

c. Philip

d. Rhosaces

269. How did Darius, king of the Persians, die?

a. He was murdered by one of his satraps

b. He fell in battle against Alexander

c. He was poisoned by his soldiers

d. None of the above

270. When did Alexander invade India?

a. 328 BC

b. 330 BC

c. 326 BC

d. 325 BC

271. In which battle did Alexander the Great defeat the local Punjab king during his invasion of India?

a. Battle of the Hydaspes River

b. Battle of Punjab

c. Battle of Homs

d. None of the above

272. During his time in Susa, what did Alexander organize to forge better relations between the Greeks and the Persians?

a. A special edition of the Olympics

b. A showcase of the Greek pantheon

c. A mass wedding between his soldiers and local Persian women

d. A tour of the famous Persian historical sites

273. In which city did Alexander die?

a. Susa

b. Persepolis

c. Babylon

d. Alexandria

274. Whose tomb did Alexander visit before his death in 326 BC?

a. Ramses II the Great

b. Cyrus the Great

c. Darius the Great

d. Philip II of Macedon

275. What was the cause of Alexander's death?

a. Malaria

b. Poisoning

c. Meningitis

d. It is unknown

ANSWERS

251. b. 336 BC

252. b. To gain wealth for himself and expand his empire's borders

253. c. Ten years

254. b. Pella

255. c. Aristotle

256. d. All of the above

257. b. 333 BC

258. c. Darius III

259. b. Thebes

260. b. League of Corinth

261. b. Granicus

262. b. 332 BC

263. b. He allowed freedom of worship

264. c. They treated Alexander as their liberator from the Persians

265. a. Ptolemy I Soter

266. a. 331 BC

267. a. Gaugamela

268. a. Cleitus

269. a. He was murdered by one of his satraps

270. c. 326 BC

271. a. Battle of the Hydaspes River

272. c. A mass wedding between his soldiers and local Persian women

273. c. Babylon

274. b. Cyrus the Great

275. d. It is unknown

The Hellenistic Period

The Hellenistic age (323–30 BC) saw the development of political thought and practice on an unprecedented scale. Ancient Greek politics and culture during this time were shaped not only by domestic developments but also by external forces. The age followed the conquests of Alexander, which spread ancient Greek culture to new boundaries. In this chapter, we'll take a look at some of the most important political, social, and cultural developments during the Hellenistic period.

276. In what series of wars were the lands of Alexander's empire divided by his generals?

a. Wars of Alexandrian succession

b. Wars of the Diadochi

c. Wars of Macedonia

d. None of the above

277. Which general emerged as the ruler of Egypt after the death of Alexander?

a. Seleucus

b. Antigonus

c. Cassander

d. Ptolemy

278. What was the largest kingdom established by one of Alexander's generals after his death?

a. Seleucid Empire

b. Kingdom of Parthia

c. Kingdom of Pontus

d. Kingdom of Pergamon

279. Why is 281 BC considered significant in terms of ancient Greek politics?

a. It marks the end of the Antigonid dynasty

b. It marks the start of a period of self-rule by Greek city-states

c. It marks Alexander III's conquest of Persia

d. It marks the end of the Wars of the Diadochi

280. What was the name of the conference held after Alexander's death where his generals addressed the matters of the empire's succession?

a. Conference of Susa

b. Partition of Babylon

c. Council of Alexandria

d. Assembly of Tarsus

281. What was the main similarity among the kingdoms established throughout the Near East after Alexander's death?

a. All kingdoms converted to Christianity

b. All kingdoms were culturally Greek

c. All kingdoms were Roman vassals

d. None of the above

282. What does the word "Hellenistic" mean?

a. Relating to Greek civilization

b. Founded by Hellena

c. Successor of the Hellas

d. All of the above

283. Which of the following statements is true about the Hellenistic period?

a. It brought about an era of increased cultural exchange

b. It led to the flourishing of trade and commerce in the Mediterranean

c. It resulted in increased migration throughout the regions

d. All of the above

284. Which city was the capital of the Seleucid Empire?

a. Jerusalem

b. Antioch

c. Alexandria

d. Tarsus

285. Which city became the largest and richest of the Mediterranean during the height of the Hellenistic period?

a. Constantinople

b. Alexandria

c. Antioch

d. Athens

286. Which of the following statements is false about the Hellenistic period?

a. The Hellenistic kingdoms coexisted in peace

b. Greek culture merged with local traditions of distant regions

c. The political importance of Greece proper declined

d. None of the above

287. What currency was most widely used by the Hellenistic world?

a. Shekel

b. Sesterius

c. Drachma

d. Denarius

288. Who made up the political elite in Hellenistic kingdoms?

a. Local elites

b. Macedonian landowners

c. Ethnic Greeks

d. The religious class

289. Where was the largest repository of knowledge located in the Hellenistic world?

a. Alexandria

b. Rome

c. Seleucia

d. Jerusalem

290. What does the term *interpretatio Graeca* refer to?

a. The efforts of Greeks to interpret local languages

b. The local interpretations of Greek institutions

c. The tendency of Greeks to identify foreign pantheons with their own

d. None of the above

291. Where was the Antigonid dynasty established after the death of Alexander the Great?

a. Parthia

b. Bactria

c. Macedon

d. Egypt

292. Which of these famous philosophers established a following during the Hellenistic period?

a. Epicurus

b. Plato

c. Socrates

d. Seneca

293. Which kingdom did the migrating Celtic peoples establish in Anatolia during the Hellenistic period?

a. Pontus

b. Bithynia

c. Galatia

d. Pergamon

294. Which Greek state emerged victorious from the Chremonidean War of 267-261 BC?

a. Sparta

b. Macedon

c. Athens

d. Corinth

295. Which Greek city-state managed to maintain independence from any of the larger Hellenistic kingdoms?

a. Rhodes

b. Trebizond

c. Pella

d. Corinth

ANSWERS

276. b. Wars of the Diadochi
277. d. Ptolemy
278. a. Seleucid Empire
279. d. It marks the end of the Wars of the Diadochi
280. b. Partition of Babylon
281. b. All kingdoms were culturally Greek
282. a. Relating to the Greek civilization
283. d. All of the above
284. b. Antioch
285. b. Alexandria
286. a. The Hellenistic kingdoms coexisted in peace
287. c. Drachma
288. c. Ethnic Greeks
289. a. Alexandria
290. c. The tendency of Greeks to identify foreign pantheons to their own
291. c. Macedon
292. a. Epicurus
293. c. Galatia
294. b. Macedon
295. a. Rhodes

Roman Conquest of Greece

The Roman conquest of Greece is one of the most interesting parts of ancient Greek history, as it resulted in the increase of Roman power in the Mediterranean and helped pave the way for Roman domination of the ancient world for the next few hundred years. In this chapter, dive deep into the intricacies of the Roman conquest of ancient Greece, from the wars fought against different configurations of Greek city-states and kingdoms to the political institutions established under Roman occupation.

296. What was the direct cause of the Battle of Corinth?

a. Dispute over territory

b. Financial disagreements

c. Political power struggles

d. Cultural differences

297. Who was the leader of the Achaean League during the Battle of Corinth?

a. Aratus of Sicyon

b. Philopoemen

c. King Philip V of Macedon

d. Diaeus

298. Which army ultimately emerged victorious in the Battle of Corinth?

a. Roman army

b. Macedonian army

c. Achaean army

d. Spartan army

299. What led to the downfall of the Achaean League?

a. Internal betrayal

b. Military defeat at the Battle of Corinth

c. Economic collapse

d. Worsening relations with Rome

300. Which Roman general led the forces against the Achaean League in the Battle of Corinth?

a. Scipio Aemilianus

b. Julius Caesar

c. Lucius Mummius

d. Quintus Marcius Philippus

301. The Battle of Corinth marks the end of what period of ancient history?

a. Golden age

b. Hellenistic age

c. Classical age

d. Mycenaean age

302. Which military tactic did the Romans utilize to defeat the Achaean phalanx?

a. Flanking maneuver

b. Cavalry charges

c. Scorching the earth

d. Naval blockade

303. What was the significance of the Battle of Corinth regarding Rome's expansion?

a. It solidified Rome's dominance over the Mediterranean region

b. It marked the beginning of Rome's decline and fall

c. It was a minor battle with no significant impact on Rome's expansion

d. It led to a split within the Roman Republic

304. Why had the Achaean League been established?

a. To counterbalance against rising Roman power

b. To counterbalance against Antigonid Macedon

c. To counterbalance against the Seleucid Empire

d. None of the above

305. Before 146 BC, who was the main ally of the Achaean League?

a. Rome

b. Carthage

c. Seleucids

d. Macedon

306. What was the aftermath of the Battle of Corinth for the city itself?

a. It was completely destroyed

b. It remained relatively unscathed

c. It was looted and plundered

d. It was left in ruins but soon rebuilt

307. When did the Macedonian Wars begin?

a. 214 BC

b. 210 BC

c. 183 BC

d. 175 BC

308. How many wars were fought in total between Rome and Macedon?

a. One

b. Two

c. Three

d. Four

309. With whom did Philip V of Macedon ally during the First Macedonian War?

a. Seleucids

b. Parthia

c. Carthage

d. Achaean League

310. Who was the king of Macedon during the First Macedonian War?

a. Alexander IV

b. Philip III

c. Philip V

d. Antigonus

311. When was Greece organized into the Roman province of Achaea?

a. 27 BC

b. 88 BC

c. 146 BC

d. 25 AD

312. What type of government system did Rome bring to ancient Greece during its occupation?

a. Monarchy

b. Republic

c. Oligarchy

d. Democracy

313. Under which emperor were the Greek lands reorganized into the province of Achaea?

a. Julius Caesar

b. Augustus

c. Marc Antony

d. Caligula

314. When was the first major rebellion against Roman rule in ancient Greece?

a. 29 AD

b. 132 AD

c. 88 BC

d. 58 BC

315. During the Roman occupation of Greece, what type of religion did they impose on the Greeks?

a. Jewish

b. Christian

c. Pagan

d. Islamic

316. Which of these can be considered the first major war between Rome and the Greek city-states?

a. First Macedonian War

b. First Punic War

c. Pyrrhic War

d. War of the Achaean League

317. After victory in which of these conflicts did the Romans nominally declare the liberation of Greece from "tyrannical Macedonian kings"?

a. First Macedonian War

b. Second Macedonian War

c. Third Macedonian War

d. Fourth Macedonian War

318. When did the Roman-Seleucid War come to an end?

a. 191 BC

b. 190 BC

c. 189 BC

d. 188 BC

319. What language was used for legal documents issued by Romans during their time in Greece?

a. Latin

b. Italian

c. Hebrew

d. Greek

320. Against which Greek city-state did Rome wage the Pyrrhic War?

a. Epirus

b. Sparta

c. Athens

d. Corinth

321. Which Roman emperor was the first to participate in the Olympic Games and was honored with victory at every contest?

a. Marcus Aurelius

b. Nero

c. Claudius

d. Theodosius

322. Which of these Roman emperors began the construction of the Roman Agora in Athens?

a. Augustus

b. Claudius

c. Julius Caesar

d. Hadrian

323. Against which Hellenistic kingdom did Rome wage the Mithridatic Wars?

a. The Seleucid Empire

b. Ptolemaic Egypt

c. Kingdom of Pontus

d. Kingdom of Parthia

324. With what treaty did the First Mithridatic War come to an end?

a. Treaty of Kadesh

b. Treaty of Dardanos

c. Treaty of Apamea

d. Treaty of Phoenice

325. Who emerged victorious from the Battle of Thermopylae in 191 BC?

a. Seleucids

b. Macedonians

c. Egyptians

d. Romans

326. What was the relation of Roman conquerors toward Greek people and culture?

a. They respected them

b. They considered them their equals

c. They wanted to undermine them

d. None of the above

327. Which of these Roman emperors briefly served as the eponymous archon of Athens?

a. Hadrian

b. Caligula

c. Vespasian

d. Trajan

328. When did the Third Mithridatic War come to an end?

   a. 73 BC

   b. 70 BC

   c. 65 BC

   d. 63 BC

329. What was the name given to large estates owned by wealthy citizens who controlled significant resources during Roman rule in Greece?

   a. Domains

   b. Latifundia

   c. Villas

   d. None of the above

330. Where is the Arch of Hadrian located?

   a. Athens

   b. Thessaloniki

   c. Rhodes

   d. Pergamon

331. Which type of philosophy became popular in Roman society during this period due to its influence from Greece?

   a. Stoicism

   b. Epicureanism

   c. Aristotelianism

   d. Platonism

332. What type of art became popular in Greco-Roman societies due to their cultural exchange?

   a. Abstract paintings

   b. Landscape drawings

   c. Sculpture

   d. Street murals

333. What form of literature was popular in this period and is still popular today?

   a. Epic poetry

   b. Dramatic plays

   c. Novels

   d. Novellas

334. **What was one characteristic of Roman high circles after the increased cultural exchange with Greece?**

a. They started to increasingly speak Greek

b. They worshipped Zeus

c. They began to emigrate to Eastern provinces

d. None of the above

335. **Which Roman emperor is famous for his contributions to Stoicism?**

a. Nero

b. Augustus

c. Trajan

d. Marcus Aurelius

ANSWERS

296. a. Dispute over territory

297. d. Diaeus

298. a. Roman army

299. d. Worsening relations with Rome

300. c. Lucius Mummius

301. b. Hellenistic age

302. a. Flanking maneuver

303. a. It solidified Rome's dominance over the Mediterranean region

304. b. To counterbalance against Antigonid Macedon

305. a. Rome

306. a. It was completely destroyed

307. a. 214 BC

308. d. Four

309. c. Carthage

310. c. Philip V

311. a. 27 BC

312. b. Republic

313. b. Augustus

314. c. 88 BC
315. c. Pagan
316. c. Pyrrhic War
317. b. Second Macedonian War
318. d. 188 BC
319. a. Latin
320. a. Epirus
321. b. Nero
322. c. Julius Caesar
323. c. Kingdom of Pontus
324. b. Treaty of Dardanos
325. d. Romans
326. a. They respected them
327. a. Hadrian
328. d. 63 BC
329. b. Latifundia
330. a. Athens
331. a. Stoicism
332. c. Sculpture
333. b. Dramatic plays
334. a. They started to increasingly speak Greek
335. d. Marcus Aurelius

Spread of Christianity

Christianity has been an indelible part of Greek culture. From ancient times, examples of incorporating elements from other religions and mythologies can be found in Greece. However, Christianity began to spread beyond its Middle Eastern birthplace and gained ground in European countries such as Greece. This chapter will explore how Christianity first entered ancient Greece, how it developed over time, and what impact it had on the Greek people living at that time.

336. According to tradition, which Christian apostle was martyred at Patras after preaching Christianity in Greece?

a. Paul

b. Thomas

c. Andrew

d. Luke

337. According to tradition, which of these cities was the first where Christianity began to spread?

a. Sparta

b. Athens

c. Philippi

d. Thessaloniki

338. According to tradition, who was Lydia of Thyatira?

    a. First bishop of Greece

    b. First convert to Christianity in Europe

    c. First woman to accept Christianity

    d. None of the above

339. What year did Emperor Constantine publicly declare his faith in Christianity and make it legal throughout the Roman Empire?

    a. 312 AD

    b. 325 AD

    c. 381 AD

    d. 1981 AD

340. When was the Edict of Milan issued?

    a. 310 AD

    b. 313 AD

    c. 315 AD

    d. 317 AD

341. According to tradition, from which Greek city did St. Paul write his epistles to the Thessalonians?

    a. Athens

    b. Corinth

    c. Sparta

    d. Thessaloniki

342. What was the purpose of the Council of Nicaea?

    a. To establish an ecumenical patriarchate

    b. To create an official creed for Christianity

    c. To spread Christianity across Europe

    d. To make Christianity legal throughout the Roman Empire

343. What happened at the Constantinople Synod (381 AD) that made it historically significant?

    a. It declared Arianism as heresy

    b. It established the Eastern Orthodox Church

    c. It recognized Pope Gregory I as leader

    d. It created an agreement between Christians and Jews

344. Which one of these early church fathers was the archbishop of Constantinople in the late fourth century?

a. Paul of Tarsus

b. John Chrysostom

c. Athanasius

d. Augustine

345. Which event helped spread Christianity all over Greek-speaking regions and made it an official religion in the fourth century AD?

a. Edict of Thessalonica

b. Council of Nicaea

c. Council of Ephesus

d. Creation of the New Testament

346. Which Roman emperor declared Christianity as the official religion of the Roman Empire?

a. Justinian

b. Constantine

c. Theodosius

d. Diocletian

347. On which of his travels did St. Paul write his second epistle to the Corinthians?

a. First missionary journey

b. Second missionary journey

c. Third missionary journey

d. Fourth missionary journey

348. According to tradition, in which Greek city did St. John the Apostle die?

a. Athens

b. Corinth

c. Thessaloniki

d. Ephesus

349. Which Roman emperor organized the Council of Nicaea?

    a. Theodosius

    b. Constantine

    c. Nero

    d. Justinian

350. Which Roman emperor was among the most vicious persecutors of Christians?

    a. Justinian

    b. Diocletian

    c. Constantine

    d. Basil

351. Which Roman emperor founded the monastery of Annesos in Pontus in 358 AD?

    a. Constantine

    b. Basil

    c. Theodosius

    d. Hadrian

352. Which of these figures is the author of *On the Holy Spirit*, written in the fourth century?

    a. Athanasius

    b. Gregory of Nyssa

    c. Basil the Great

    d. Gregory the Theologian

353. Where were the relics of John Chrysostom buried?

    a. Constantinople

    b. Thessaloniki

    c. Athens

    d. Ephesus

354. When did the Council of Chalcedon take place?

    a. 450 AD

    b. 464 AD

    c. 451 AD

    d. 497 AD

355. Which of the apostles is believed to have visited Athens, according to tradition?

a. Thomas

b. Peter

c. Judas

d. Paul

ANSWERS

336. c. Andrew

337. c. Philippi

338. b. First convert to Christianity in Europe

339. a. 312 AD

340. b. 313 AD

341. b. Corinth

342. b. To create an official creed of Christianity

343. a. It declared Arianism as heresy

344. b. John Chrysostom

345. a. Edict of Thessalonica

346. c. Theodosius

347. c. Third missionary journey

348. d. Ephesus

349. b. Constantine

350. b. Diocletian

351. b. Basil

352. c. Basil the Great

353. a. Constantinople

354. c. 451 AD

355. d. Paul

The Byzantine Empire in Ancient Greece and Justinian's Reign

Explore the captivating and complex history of ancient Greece during Justinian's reign with this chapter. Test your knowledge of the once-mighty empire by answering questions about Emperor Justinian's military forces, primary sources of income, government bureaucracy, artistry and engineering feats, legal reforms, and diplomatic rituals. Understand how the empress assisted her husband's rule, as well as the importance of fortifications along major points in Europe like the Danube River to fend off foreign invasions. Make sure you can express what caused the decline of the Byzantine Empire after Justinian's death, among many other topics.

356. During Justinian's reign, what was the official language of the Byzantine Empire?

a. Latin

b. Greek

c. Aramaic

d. Hebrew

357. Who is credited with codifying Roman law during Justinian's rule?

a. Constantine I

b. Philip II

c. Heraclius

d. Justinian I

358. How did Emperor Justinian initially strengthen his military forces?

a. He hired mercenaries to fight for him

b. He built large fortresses to protect against invaders

c. He recruited soldiers from local communities

d. He increased taxes on citizens to pay for more troops

359. During Justinian's reign, what was the primary source of income for the Byzantine Empire?

a. Farming and agriculture

b. Trade and commerce

c. Taxation and tribute

d. Mining

360. How did Justinian improve government bureaucracy during his rule?

a. He created positions based on merit rather than birthright

b. He abolished all public offices except for those of tax collectors

c. He created an imperial court to oversee local administration

d. He appointed provincial governors with absolute authority

361. What were the two major accomplishments of Emperor Justinian in terms of artistry and engineering?

a. Building Hagia Sophia and constructing aqueducts

b. Commissioning mosaics and developing new irrigation systems

c. Constructing fortresses and expanding trade routes

d. Establishing religious schools and creating libraries

362. Who was the empress of the Byzantine Empire during Justinian's reign?

a. Theodora

b. Irene

c. Helena

d. Zoe

363. When did Justinian become emperor of the Byzantine Empire?

a. 476 AD

b. 527 AD

c. 602 AD

d. 717 AD

364. **What were the two major accomplishments of Emperor Justinian regarding law and justice?**

a. He codified Roman law and established an autocratic government

b. He created an imperial court system and reformed the legal code

c. He abolished all public offices except tax collectors

d. He appointed provincial governors with absolute authority

365. **What type of art flourished during Justinian's rule in the Byzantine Empire?**

a. Mosaics

b. Frescoes

c. Sculptures

d. Woodcarving

366. **How did the Byzantine Empire fare economically during Justinian's rule?**

a. The economy thrived, with improvements to agriculture, manufacturing, and trading

b. The economy declined due to high taxes imposed by the emperor

c. The economy stagnated as resources were diverted toward military campaigns

d. The economy remained stagnant due to weak central leadership

367. **Who was the most powerful general during Justinian's reign?**

a. Belisarius

b. Phocas

c. Heraclius

d. Constantine I

368. **How did Emperor Justinian attempt to reunite the Eastern Orthodox Church under one ruler?**

a. He declared himself as head of all religious institutions

b. He used military force to subjugate religious dissenters

c. He issued an edict that prohibited worship outside of Constantinople

d. He established diplomatic relations with other Christian empires

369. How did Emperor Justinian use diplomacy to maintain peace in the Mediterranean region?

a. He formed alliances with other empires

b. He negotiated peace treaties with neighboring countries

c. He increased naval presence in the Mediterranean Sea

d. He imposed tariffs on incoming goods from foreign powers

370. How did Empress Theodora help Emperor Justinian's reign?

a. She supported his policies on religious unity

b. She funded scientific research to advance education

c. She wrote laws that granted women more rights

d. She built monuments throughout Constantinople

ANSWERS

356. b. Greek

357. d. Justinian I

358. c. He recruited soldiers from local communities

359. b. Trade and commerce

360. a. He created positions based on merit rather than birthright

361. a. Building Hagia Sophia and constructing aqueducts

362. a. Theodora

363. b. 527 AD

364. b. He created an imperial court system and reformed the legal code

365. a. Mosaics

366. a. The economy thrived, with improvements in agriculture, manufacturing, and trading

367. a. Belisarius

368. d. He established diplomatic relations with other Christian empires

369. b. He negotiated peace treaties with neighboring countries

370. c. She wrote laws that granted women more rights

Religion and Mythology

Explore the mysterious roots of ancient Greek religion and mythology in this chapter, from questioning who was the father of the gods to discovering an oracle at Delphi with seemingly prophetic powers. The myths tell of divine figures like Zeus, wielding lightning bolts; Athena, born out of a sea goddess' head fully grown and armed with weapons; and Poseidon, punishing heroes. Learn more about these wondrous tales that have been passed down through the generations, including symbols associated with each god or goddess and heavily debated questions that persist today. Test your knowledge of various creatures while also studying gods associated with certain elements. Finally, solve puzzles related not just to religious functions but to understanding the mysteries of ancient Greek religion and mythology.

371. According to Greek mythology, which figure was the god of wine?

   a. Zeus

   b. Dionysus

   c. Apollo

   d. Poseidon

372. Which goddess was known as the protector of Athens?

   a. Athena

   b. Aphrodite

   c. Hestia

   d. Artemis

373. What is the name of the oracle at Delphi who could interpret signs from the gods?

a. Cassandra

b. Hera

c. Pythia

d. Demeter

374. What type of half-man/half-horse creatures were believed to have been ridden by heroes such as Bellerophon in Greek mythological stories?

a. Centaurs

b. Minotaurs

c. Gryphons

d. Pegasus

375. Who were Scylla and Charybdis in Greek mythology?

a. Sister sirens

b. Monsters encountered by Odysseus

c. Two lost daughters of Zeus

d. None of the above

376. In Greek mythology, who is known as the god of metalworking?

a. Hera

b. Hephaestus

c. Aphrodite

d. Demeter

377. According to Greek legend, which figure tricked Persephone into eating pomegranate seeds, causing her to spend half of each year in the underworld?

a. Zeus

b. Heracles

c. Hermes

d. Hades

378. Who were the three goddesses that symbolized fate and destiny in ancient Greece?

a. Clotho, Lachesis, and Atropos

b. Athena, Artemis, and Apollo

c. Hera, Hestia, and Eileithyia

d. Demeter, Dionysius, and Pan

379. Which mythological creature had wings like an eagle, the face of a woman, and a lion's body?

a. Sphinx

b. Minotaur

c. Centaur

d. Harpy

380. Who was the Greek goddess of marriage and childbirth?

a. Aphrodite

b. Hestia

c. Hera

d. Demeter

381. According to mythological stories, who is Apollo's twin sister?

a. Artemis

b. Athena

c. Hera

d. Aphrodite

382. In ancient Greece religion, what sacred object did Zeus carry in his hand as he traveled around Mount Olympus?

a. A lightning bolt

b. An olive branch

c. A bow and arrow

d. A golden harp

383. What animal did Zeus transform himself into when seducing Leda according to legend?

a. Swan

b. Bull

c. Tiger

d. Dragon

384. Which figure from Greek mythology stole fire from Mount Olympus so that humans could use it on Earth?

a. Prometheus

b. Zeus

c. Apollo

d. Heracles

385. What is the name of a priest or priestess in ancient Greece responsible for interpreting signs from the gods?

a. Oracle

b. Prophet

c. Shaman

d. Seer

386. Who is known as the goddess of wisdom in Greek mythology?

a. Hera

b. Artemis

c. Athena

d. Demeter

387. In Greek mythology, what type of creature had wings like an eagle, claws like a lion, and body parts like various other animals such as serpents and goats?

a. Sphinx

b. Chimera

c. Harpy

d. Minotaur

388. According to Greek mythology, who was Cronos (Kronos)?

a. Brother of Poseidon

b. Titan father of Zeus

c. The god of earth

d. None of the above

389. According to ancient Greek mythology, what was Tartarus?

a. A dark dungeon

b. The birthplace of Hades

c. Poseidon's underwater castle

d. None of the above

390. According to ancient Greek mythology, which ancient creatures were the spirits of the trees?

a. Satyrs

b. Nereids

c. Dryads

d. Nymphs

391. Who was the son of Heracles, according to ancient Greek mythology?

a. Perseus

b. Theseus

c. Telephus

d. Prometheus

392. According to ancient Greek mythology, where was the one weakness of Achilles?

a. His neck

b. His heel

c. His armpit

d. His knee

393. Who was the mother of Achilles?

a. Athena

b. Nike

c. Thetis

d. Demeter

394. To which ancient kingdom did the Argonautic expedition travel?

a. Egypt

b. Seleucia

c. Carthage

d. Colchis

395. According to tradition, which hero defeated the minotaur?

a. Theseus

b. Perseus

c. Heracles

d. Deucalion

396. Which of these figures from Greek mythology was a legendary musician and a poet?

a. Apollo

b. Orpheus

c. Hermes

d. Pan

397. According to Greek mythology, which god invented the lyre?

a. Hermes

b. Apollo

c. Athena

d. Orpheus

398. Which god defeated Cronus and put an end to the age of the Titans in Greek mythology?

a. Gaia

b. Hades

c. Ares

d. Zeus

399. Who was the patron deity for the Parthenon?

a. Athena

b. Poseidon

c. Apollo

d. Demeter

ANSWERS

371. b. Dionysus
372. a. Athena
373. c. Pythia
374. a. Centaurs
375. b. Two monsters encountered by Odysseus
376. b. Hephaestus
377. d. Hades
378. a. Clotho, Lachesis, and Atropos
379. a. Sphinx
380. c. Hera
381. a. Artemis
382. a. A lightning bolt
383. a. Swan
384. a. Prometheus
385. a. Oracle
386. c. Athena
387. b. Chimera
388. b. Titan father of Zeus
389. a. A dark dungeon
390. c. Dryads
391. c. Telephus
392. b. His heel
393. c. Thetis
394. d. Colchis
395. a. Theseus
396. b. Orpheus
397. a. Hermes
398. d. Zeus
399. a. Athena

Philosophy

From the birth of philosophy with Thales and Pythagoras to its development through Plato, Socrates, Aristotle, Heraclitus, and ultimately into schools like Epicureanism, Stoicism, and Cynicism, ancient Greece was home to some of the greatest minds in history. This chapter on philosophy will ask you questions about these key figures' lives, teachings, and writings. You'll also explore vital theories such as Forms and sophistry, among others. Let's begin this journey by exploring ancient Greek philosophy.

400. What ancient Greek philosopher wrote the *Republic*?

a. Plato

b. Aristotle

c. Socrates

d. Pythagoras

401. Whose disciple was Plato?

a. Pythagoras

b. Aristotle

c. Thales

d. Socrates

402. Which school of philosophy held that reality was composed solely of matter and energy and everything else is an illusion?

a. Stoicism

b. Epicureanism

c. Materialism

d. Pantheism

403. From which city was Thales, considered one of the first Greek philosophers?

a. Athens

b. Corinth

c. Miletus

d. Knossos

404. According to Thales, what was the source from which all other things are derived?

a. Love

b. Water

c. Justice

d. Wisdom

405. Who proposed the doctrine of the immortality of the soul?

a. Plato

b. Aristotle

c. Socrates

d. Pythagoras

406. What is the name of the school of philosophy founded by Zeno in Athens?

a. Epicureanism

b. Cynicism

c. Stoicism

d. Platonism

407. Which ancient Greek philosopher was known for his theory of Forms?

a. Heraclitus

b. Ammonius Saccas

c. Parmenides

d. Plato

408. Which of these philosophers is considered the main proponent of cynicism?

a. Diogenes

b. Pythagoras

c. Democritus

d. Empedocles

409. Which two philosophers are often referred to as the founders of

Western philosophy?

a. Socrates and Plato

b. Thales and Euclid

c. Homer and Hesiod

d. Aristotle and Zeno

410. According to which philosophical school should one live life in harmony with nature's laws and human nature itself?

a. Epicureanism

b. Stoicism

c. Cynicism

d. Platonism

411. Who was the first philosopher to attempt a systematic study of nature?

a. Plato

b. Thales

c. Aristotle

d. Socrates

412. What did Democritus believe were the fundamental building blocks of all matter?

a. Atoms

b. Molecules

c. Quarks

d. Particles

413. The proponents of which philosophical school advocated for hedonism and pleasure as the ultimate goal of life?

a. Epicureanism

b. Stoicism

c. Cynicism

d. Cyrenaicism

414. Who is credited as the father of logic in Western philosophy?

a. Anaximenes

b. Parmenides

c. Zeno of Elea

d. Aristotle

415. What does sophistry refer to in ancient Greek philosophy?

    a. The use of clever but false arguments

    b. The process of endless deliberation

    c. The use of moral relativism

    d. None of the above

416. Which of these philosophers accompanied Alexander the Great to India?

    a. Democritus

    b. Pyrrho of Elis

    c. Epicurus

    d. Aristotle

417. What did Heraclitus believe is the fundamental element in nature?

    a. Air

    b. Fire

    c. Water

    d. Earth

418. Which of these philosophical schools influenced the development of Christianity?

    a. Epicureanism

    b. Stoicism

    c. Cynicism

    d. Neoplatonism

ANSWERS

400. a. Plato

401. d. Socrates

402. c. Materialism

403. c. Miletus

404. b. Water

405. a. Plato

406. c. Stoicism

407. d. Plato

408. a. Diogenes

409. a. Socrates and Plato

410. b. Stoicism

411. b. Thales

412. a. Atoms

413. d. Cyrenaicism

414. d. Aristotle

415. a. The use of clever but false arguments

416. b. Pyrrho of Elis

417. b. Fire

418. d. Neoplatonism

Art and Culture

The art and culture of ancient Greece were spectacularly influential over the centuries, including our own. This chapter will test your knowledge of the major contributions this civilization has made to us by asking questions about famous politicians, architecture, artwork, and more. With questions from which material most sculptures were made out of during the classical period to who designed the infamous Trojan Horse, it's time to find out just how well you know ancient Greek trivia.

419. Who is considered the greatest Athenian statesman?

    a. Cicero

    b. Cleisthenes

    c. Pericles

    d. Aristotle

420. What is a common element of ancient Greek architecture?

    a. Columns

    b. Arches

    c. Stucco

    d. Domes

421. How did the ancient Greeks view art and aesthetics?

    a. Art was seen as an important part of everyday life

    b. Art was only appreciated by wealthy citizens

    c. Art had no purpose in society

    d. None of the above

422. Where is the Temple of Athena Nike located?

    a. Thessaloniki

    b. Rhodes

    c. Athens

    d. None of the above

423. What material were most sculptures made out of during the classical period?

    a. Marble

    b. Bronze

    c. Wood

    d. Clay

424. Who is the author of the tragedy *Bacchae*?

    a. Aristophanes

    b. Euripides

    c. Plato

    d. Diogenes

425. Which of these ancient Greek playwrights was a comedian?

    a. Euripides

    b. Sophocles

    c. Agathon

    d. Aristophanes

426. Which of these is a characteristic of ancient Greek sculpture?

    a. Elements of realism

    b. Depictions of gods from mythology

    c. Monumentalism

    d. All of the above

427. In which famous museum is the sculpture *Winged Victory of Samothrace* located?

    a. Louvre

    b. British Museum

    c. Palazzo Massimo

    d. Metropolitan Museum

428. When did Classical Greece reach its peak in terms of cultural and political power?

a. Fifth century BC

b. Tenth century BC

c. Fifteenth century BC

d. Twentieth century AD

429. Who designed the famous Trojan Horse, as told in Homer's *Iliad*?

a. Odysseus

b. Paris

c. Achilles

d. Hector

430. Who wrote *Oedipus Rex*, one of ancient Greece's most iconic plays?

a. Homer

b. Euripides

c. Sophocles

d. Plato

431. Which of these is not an example of ancient Greek architecture?

a. Parthenon

b. Temple of Zeus

c. Acropolis

d. Colosseum

432. Which of these statements is true about ancient Greek theater?

a. Actors usually performed multiple roles in each play

b. There were only male actors

c. Only a few actors were allowed on stage at a time

d. All of the above

433. What was the most popular form of theater in ancient Greece?

a. Comedy

b. Tragedy

c. Opera

d. Ballet

434. Which of these is not a play by Sophocles?

a. Oedipus Rex

b. Antigone

c. Medea

d. Ajax

435. How did the Parthenon differ from other temples in ancient Greece?

a. It was made entirely out of marble

b. It served as a treasury

c. It was dedicated to Athena

d. It was smaller than other temples

436. Which later artistic movement was greatly influenced by classical styles?

a. Avant-garde

b. Renaissance

c. Medieval

d. Impressionism

437. Which of these is not considered a part of the "Theban plays" by Sophocles?

a. Oedipus Rex

b. Oedipus at Colone

c. Antigone

d. Ajax

ANSWERS

419. c. Pericles
420. a. Columns
421. a. Art was seen as an important part of everyday life
422. c. Athens
423. a. Marble
424. b. Euripides
425. d. Aristophanes
426. d. All of the above
427. a. Louvre
428. a. Fifth century BC
429. a. Odysseus
430. c. Sophocles
431. d. Colosseum
432. d. All of the above
433. b. Tragedy
434. c. Medea
435. b. It served as a treasury
436. b. Renaissance
437. d. Ajax

Mathematics and Science

Take a journey through the centuries and explore the remarkable contributions of ancient Greece's mathematicians and scientists. From mathematical circles to medical mysteries, there is no shortage of winsome artifacts that survived this world-renowned civilization. Test your knowledge of integral calculus or atomic theory in this chapter full of entertaining ancient Greek trivia on mathematics and science.

438. Which ancient Greek figure is considered the "inventor" of geometry?

a. Euclid

b. Socrates

c. Plato

d. Pythagoras

439. Who wrote *The History of Animals*, which focuses on zoology and natural history?

a. Archimedes

b. Galen

c. Plato

d. Aristotle

440. Which ancient Greek scientist is considered the inventor of trigonometry?

a. Euclid

b. Hipparchus

c. Aristotle

d. Hippocrates

441. Which ancient Greek poet worked on a new calendar system that would better regulate the change of seasons and the appearance of different stars as early as ca. 700 BC?

a. Agathon

b. Hesiod

c. Nossis

d. Homer

442. Who wrote *Physics*, which focuses on natural philosophy and cosmology?

a. Euclid

b. Archimedes

c. Aristotle

d. Plato

443. Which Greek scientist managed to calculate Earth's circumference with remarkable accuracy in the third century BC?

a. Aristotle

b. Ptolemy

c. Eratosthenes

d. Archimedes

444. Which influential scientist developed theories about the movement of celestial bodies around the Earth?

a. Eratosthenes

b. Galen

c. Kepler

d. Ptolemy

445. What did Thales of Miletus famously prove that helped establish mathematics as a field of study in ancient Greece?

a. The eclipses

b. The tides

c. Earthquake timing

d. Triangles' angles

446. What is the Antikythera mechanism commonly referred to?

    a. First mechanical computer

    b. First Greek calendar

    c. First robot

    d. First water wheel

447. Who developed a method for finding prime numbers that now bears his name?

    a. Archimedes

    b. Heron

    c. Euclid

    d. Eratosthenes

448. Which ancient Greek mathematician is credited with inventing the theorem to find the sides of a right triangle?

    a. Democritus

    b. Pythagoras

    c. Euclid

    d. Eratosthenes

449. Who discovered the principle behind hydrostatics by noting that water in an open container always seeks its own level?

    a. Democritus

    b. Heron of Alexandria

    c. Archimedes

    d. Hippocrates

450. Whose works provide one of the earliest propositions and proofs of the mathematical concept known as the Golden Ratio?

    a. Euclid

    b. Thales

    c. Pythagoras

    d. Aristotle

ANSWERS

438. a. Euclid

439. d. Aristotle

440. b. Hipparchus

441. b. Hesiod

442. c. Aristotle

443. c. Eratosthenes

444. d. Ptolemy

445. d. Triangles' angles

446. a. First mechanical computer

447. d. Eratosthenes

448. b. Pythagoras

449. c. Archimedes

450. a. Euclid

Conclusion

Ancient Greece Trivia has taken its readers on a journey through the history and culture of one of the most influential civilizations in human history.

Covering every period from the Minoan civilization to Justinian's reign, this book has detailed significant events like the Greco-Persian Wars, the Peloponnesian War, and Alexander's conquests, as well as important contributions made by Greeks in fields such as religion and mythology, philosophy, Greek art and culture, mathematics, and science.

Throughout this journey, we have seen how ancient Greece was at the forefront of innovations that shaped our world today, from building projects under Pericles' rule to the development of the alphabet, which ultimately led to the spread of literacy throughout Europe.

This book has detailed significant events in ancient Greek history that have contributed to shaping what we know today as "Western civilization." It is indeed an ode to ancient Greece and its people, who have left an indelible mark on humanity through their contributions in multiple fields.

Check out another book in the series

Welcome Aboard, Check Out This Limited-Time Free Bonus!

Ahoy, reader! Welcome to the Ahoy Publications family, and thanks for snagging a copy of this book! Since you've chosen to join us on this journey, we'd like to offer you something special.

Check out the link below for a FREE e-book filled with delightful facts about American History.

But that's not all - you'll also have access to our exclusive email list with even more free e-books and insider knowledge. Well, what are ye waiting for? Click the link below to join and set sail toward exciting adventures in American History.

Access your bonus here

https://ahoypublications.com/

Or, Scan the QR code!

www.ingramcontent.com/pod-product-compliance
Lightning Source LLC
Chambersburg PA
CBHW070724130626
46553CB00005B/2144